Texts from Mittens

Texts from Mittens

A Cat Who Has an Unlimited Data Plan… and Isn't Afraid to Use It

Angie Bailey

HANOVER
SQUARE
PRESS™

HANOVER
SQUARE
PRESS™

Texts from Mittens:
A Cat Who Has an Unlimited Data Plan…
and Isn't Afraid to Use it

ISBN-13: 978-1-335-47405-6

First published in 2015. This edition published in 2021 with revised text.

This edition published
by arrangement with
Harlequin Books S.A.

Hanover Square Press
22 Adelaide St. West, 40th Floor
Toronto, Ontario M5H 4E3, Canada
HanoverSqPress.com
BookClubbish.com

Printed in Italy

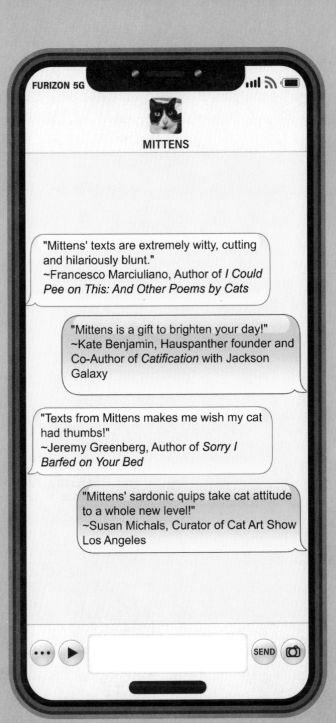

MITTENS

"Mittens' texts are extremely witty, cutting and hilariously blunt."
~Francesco Marciuliano, Author of *I Could Pee on This: And Other Poems by Cats*

"Mittens is a gift to brighten your day!"
~Kate Benjamin, Hauspanther founder and Co-Author of *Catification* with Jackson Galaxy

"Texts from Mittens makes me wish my cat had thumbs!"
~Jeremy Greenberg, Author of *Sorry I Barfed on Your Bed*

"Mittens' sardonic quips take cat attitude to a whole new level!"
~Susan Michals, Curator of Cat Art Show Los Angeles

SEND

CHARACTER GUIDE

Mittens:
A text-happy, indoor tuxie who loves *Judge Judy,* liver treats, fancy drinking fountains and creating unnecessary drama.

Mom:
A single, working woman who loves puns and dabbles in online dating. She (usually) sees through Mittens' schemes and supplies the treats.

Phil:
The Lab-mix "filthy hound" who lives with Mittens and Mom. He constantly irritates Mittens just by "being Phil."

Stumpy:
Mittens' wild best friend who lives down the block. A large, indoor-outdoor, orange tabby who visits Mittens to watch TV, eat treats and enjoy (lots of) catnip.

Grandma:
The bearer of fancy food and presents. Mittens makes special allowances for Grandma when it comes to taking photos, wearing costumes and participating in other degrading activities.

Drunk Patty:
The usually tipsy, tacky, next-door neighbor who adores Mittens and feeds him and Phil when Mom is gone. Mittens is annoyed by everything that is Drunk Patty.

2

3

Waiting for an apology.

Why?

You locked me out of the bathroom.

I was showering.

But didn't you hear me pounding?

I was showering.

"I was showering" is not an apology.

SEND

FURIZON 5G

MITTENS

You're not clipping my claws tonight. They make me look fierce!

Yes I am.

Manicures are not fierce.

I'll fluff you so you look imposing.

You know very little of fierceness.

SEND

8

11

12

13

14

15

16

17

18

19

20

22

Left phone (MITTENS):

A bird flew into the patio door and looks dead. Can I have him?

No.

I never get to do anything exotic!

How about those banjo-shaped treats Grandma brought you from Dollywood?

Oh, that's exotic. Let me make sure I have my passport.

Right phone (MITTENS):

I'm napping in 5 minutes.

What?

I'm texting you my activities. It's like a peek into my diary.

Now I'm drinking from my fancy fountain.

Just catch me up tonight, Mitty.

Dear Diary: No one cares. I am an island.

27

28

29

30

31

32

33

35

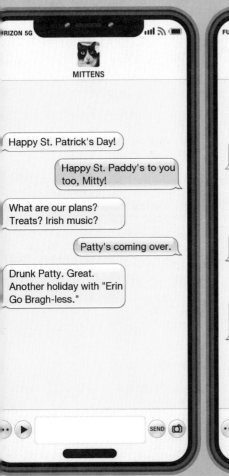

37

38

39

40

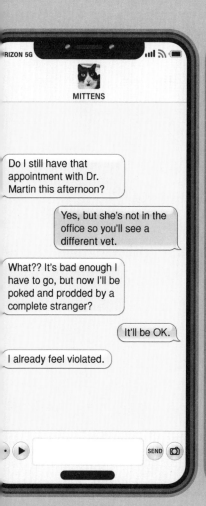

41

42

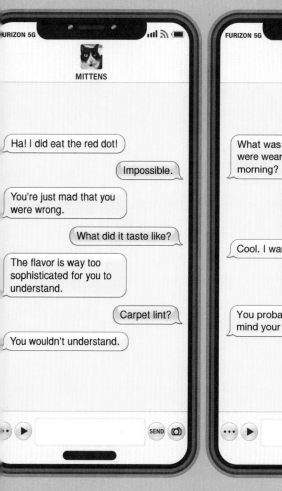

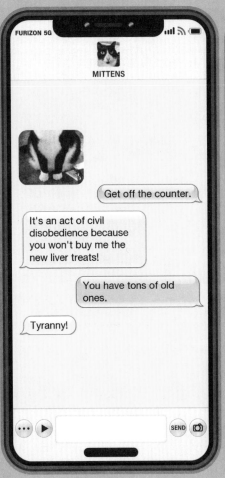

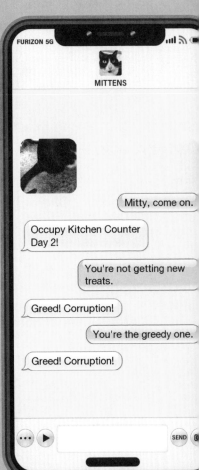

45

48

50

54

57

58

59

60

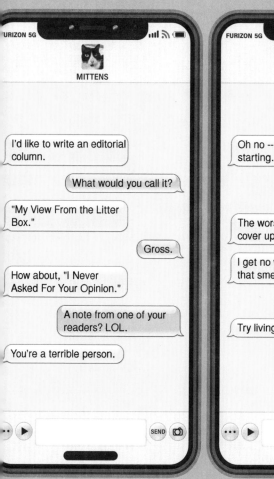

63

65

70

71

72

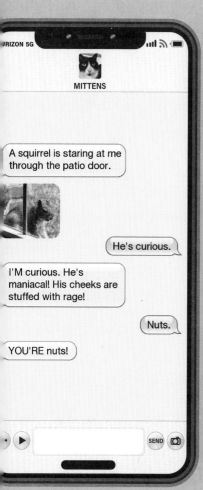

73

74

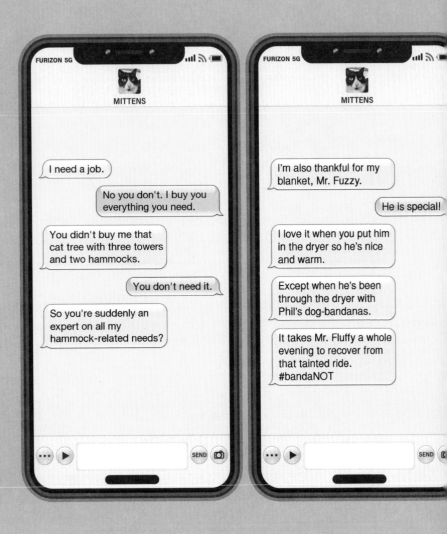

78

79

80

81

82

83

85

91

93

97

98

CREDITS

Kari, Darrell and Drake Osment: pages vi, 7, 10, 17, 22, 34, 38, 44, 58, 65

Angie Bailey: pages vi, vii, 24, 28, 48, 77, 82, 83, 89, 91

Katy Herman: pages vi, vii, 4, 20, 51, 67

Kari Achenbach: page vii, 13

Toni Nicholson: page 74

Hank Elzweig: page 57

The following images originally appeared on Catster.com: pages 1a, 6ab, 7b, 9ab, 11ab, 12ab, 13a, 15ab, 17b, 18a, 21a, 25b, 26a, 29a, 31ab, 32a, 34a, 46b, 50a, 53a, 59b, 60a, 61a, 64ab, 68b, 69a, 72b, 73ab, 76b, 77a, 78a, 80b, 84a, 88b, 90b, 95b

ACKNOWLEDGMENTS

Texts from Mittens wouldn't have been possible without the ongoing support of my friends at Catster.com, from where the column originated. Endless gratitude to you for taking a chance on Mitty!

Much gratitude to the *Texts from Mittens* online readers, whose love of a neurotic feline character and his wacky world make my heart sing. I love laughing with you every day!

Thank you to Jay Harris and his wild creativity skills for creating the initial Mittens digital image.

A lot of this craziness wouldn't have been possible without the ongoing collaboration of Katy Herman, Kari Achenbach, and Kari, Darrell and Drake Osment: Your patience and willingness to set up and take endless (sometimes strange) photos is golden. And of course, lots of ear-scritches and head-butts to Bullet, Ivan and Bombur.

Thanks to Becca Hunt, my cat-crazy editor at Harlequin. You made the entire experience so extraordinarily fun and delightfully seamless. Thanks to Fiona Cunningham, whose contagious enthusiasm makes her the perfect digital marketing manager for Mittens.

Once again, my agent Sorche Fairbank of Fairbank Literary Representation and I teamed up to share ridiculous cat humor with the world. You continue to be the most fantastic partner any cat-loving writer could hope for, and the best agent *ever*! Not even kidding.

And, of course, thank you to my friends and family (human and feline), who constantly encourage me, love me and allow me to immerse myself in the world of Mittens.